Don't Stomp on That Bug!

Holly Hartman

Contents

Rigby®

A Harcourt Achieve Imprint

www.Rigby.com
1-800-531-5015

Look! There's a bug crawling by your shoe!

2

What will you do?

Will you stomp on it, startle it, or just study it a bit?

The whole world needs bugs.

Bugs are food for fish, frogs, birds, and other animals. Without bugs to eat, many animals would die.

Plants need pollen to make seeds. Bugs carry the pollen from plant to plant. Without bugs, we would not have flowers and many fruits and vegetables.

Bugs help in other ways, too.

How do ants help?

Ants move dirt.

As ants make their tunnels, they plow up mountains of dirt. This makes spaces under the ground. Then air and water can get to the roots of plants. Most plants grow stronger when their roots are in loose dirt.

How do beetles help?

Beetles recycle!

Beetles munch on dead plants and animals. As beetles eat dead things, they clean up the ground. The things they eat are turned into new food for plants.

How do dragonflies help?

Dragonflies eat nasty bugs.

Dragonflies eat many of the bugs that bother people, like flies and mosquitoes. Flies and mosquitoes carry germs that can make us sick. As dragonflies eat these bugs, they keep germs from spreading.

How do honeybees help?

Honeybees make honey and wax.

The bees make honey to feed their queen bee. Honey is a good food that people and animals also like to eat.

The bees make wax to store their honey. Wax from beehives is used to make candles.

How do ladybugs help?

Ladybugs protect plants.

Tiny bugs called aphids can kill plants. Ladybugs eat lots of aphids.

How do silkworms help?

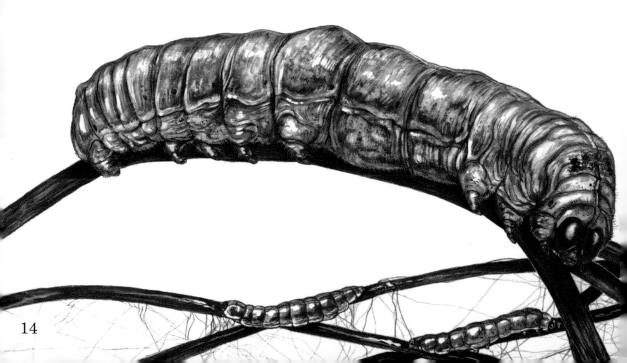

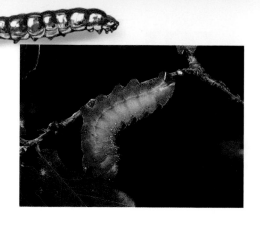

Silkworm caterpillars spin silk.

People use silk to make clothes. Silk is a very soft and smooth cloth. Some people raise silkworms and sell the silk to make money.

Look! That bug is still by your shoe. What will you do?